smart girl's GUIDE

MAKING A DIFFERENCE

using your talents and passions to change the world

by Melissa Seymour
illustrated by Stevie Lewis

Published by American Girl Publishing

20 21 22 23 24 25 26 QP 10 9 8 7 6 5 4 3 2 1

Editorial Development: Melissa Hammond, Barbara Stretchberry
Art Direction and Design: Jessica Rogers
Illustrations: Stevie Lewis
Production: Jessica Bernard, Caryl Boyer, Kristi Lively, Cynthia Stiles
Special thanks to Hannah Gómez

Cataloging-in-Publication Data available from the Library of Congress

Dear Reader,

Did you know YOU have the power to make a difference in the world? That can mean a lot of things: volunteering at an animal shelter, sitting by someone eating lunch alone at school, organizing a fund-raiser for a cause near and dear to your heart, or speaking up when something doesn't feel quite right.

Sometimes it's hard to know where to begin because creating positive change can feel like a big, confusing goal to tackle. This book will help you identify your talents and passions and then guide you to use them to change the world, your community, and even your day-to-day life at home and at school. Use these tools to gain the confidence to march forward and stand up for the issues that light a spark in you.

Now more than ever, girls just like you are speaking up and making the world a better place. Keep reading and you'll discover how you can be a changemaker (someone making a positive difference), which issues mean the most to you and why, what your strengths are when it comes to taking action, and how you can jump in and start making change right now. You'll be introduced to lots of incredible girls just like you who are changing the world in big and small ways. From caring for animals, to protecting the planet, to helping people far away or right in your community, there are so many ways to make a difference.

Are you ready? Let's get started, changemakers!

Your friends at American Girl

contents

be the change 6

the ripple effect 8

start with heart 10

check it out

changemaker's notebook

what's activism?

Quiz: how to help?

game-changing girls

empathy, always

caring for a cause 28

what's important to you?

beyond the bubble

discover more

what are you passionate about?

study up!

getting started 42

one action at a time

small actions, BIG changes

Quiz: where in the world?

a helping hand 56

volunteering

raising awareness

donating

how to start a collection

fund-raising

raise money creatively

Quiz: ready . . . action!

easing your worries . . .78

where to start?

take care of you, too

the future is yours 86

dream big

get started!

dive in

be the change

So, you want to make a difference? Great! Everything you need to change the world is already inside you.

Maybe you're here because you feel a little flicker of joy inside when you help others.

No matter the reason, you want to make the world a better place. Let's get to work!

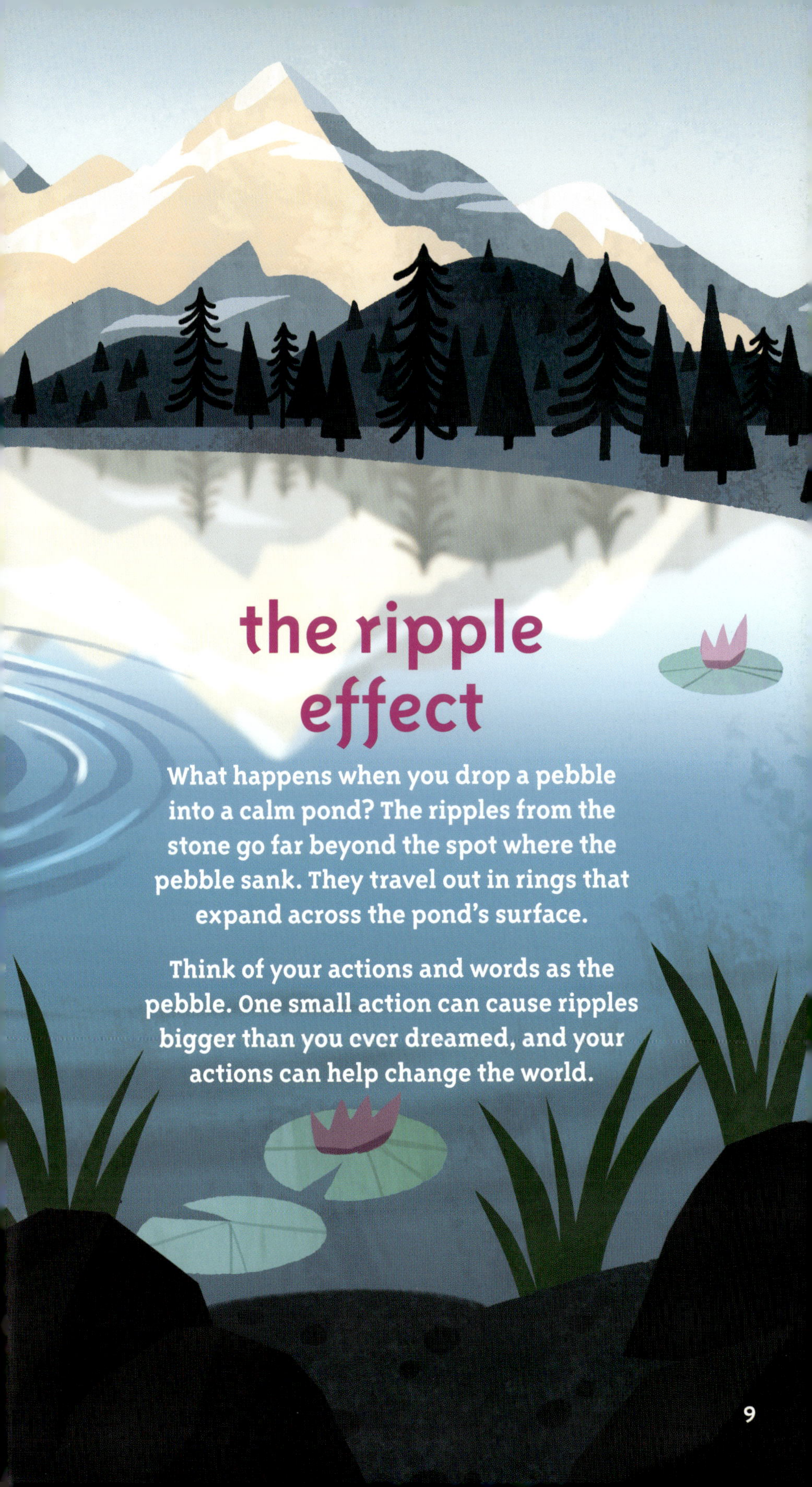

the ripple effect

What happens when you drop a pebble into a calm pond? The ripples from the stone go far beyond the spot where the pebble sank. They travel out in rings that expand across the pond's surface.

Think of your actions and words as the pebble. One small action can cause ripples bigger than you ever dreamed, and your actions can help change the world.

NIMAL SHELTER
ANIMAL SHELTE
ADOPT A PET IN NEED
ANIMAL SHELTER

START WITH HEART

check it out

Why do you want to change the world? What does that pebble mean to you? Put a check next to each statement that feels right. Knowing why you want to make a difference can help you figure out what causes to dedicate your time and energy to.

☐ Helping others makes me feel really happy.

☐ I want to be part of a community that matters to me.

☐ I like using my voice to lift others up.

☐ I want to be a leader.

☐ Speaking out about important issues makes me feel confident and strong.

- [x] I want to make the world a better place.
- [x] I like teaching others.

- [ ] Helping gives me a sense of purpose.
- [ ] I want to learn more about my community and the world.

- [x] I want my community to be safe for everyone.

All these reasons are worthwhile, and they might change as you grow. Do you have any other reasons for wanting to help? Jot them down in a notebook and keep it nearby. The statements you checked will help you decide what to focus on and how you'll make positive change in the world.

changemaker's notebook

It can be helpful to keep all your notes, ideas, and research in one place. Fill your changemaker's notebook with questions, concerns, and facts you learn about the issue you're researching. This is a great place to begin jotting down ideas or plans about how you'll take action.

Other things to put in your notebook:

Clippings from magazines, articles, and posters

Inspirational sayings that motivate you

Pictures of leaders you look up to

Sketches or doodles that relate to the cause you care about

Quotes from blogs or podcasts

"Mother Earth doesn't need us, but we need her."
– Autumn Peltier

Facts that relate to the cause

73: percent of beach litter that is plastic

450: number of years it takes for a plastic bottle to decompose

12: number of minutes a plastic bag is in use

what's activism?

Activism =
bringing change to an issue or problem in the world, your community, or your life.

An activist =
someone helping to change an issue that's important to them.

owledge
is
OWER
Girls deserve the same rights as BOYS
Support Girls' Education
Educate GIRLS 4 success
EDUCATION FOR ALL
"Principal Hale, switching to reusable plates in the cafeteria would be awesome for the environment. Is this something we can talk about?"
Principal Hale

Quiz

how to help?

Take this quiz to discover how your strengths and talents can help you make a difference.

1. You can't find your book *Out of This World: Famous Women Astronauts* anywhere. You . . .

a. ask your family if they've seen it—maybe your brother borrowed it again?

b. retrace your steps and make a list of the places you read it last.

c. spend the afternoon sketching portraits of the women featured in the book.

2. What's inside your locker?

a. A photo from the Halloween party you and your BFF planned—your costume was hilarious.

b. A cozy sweater for chilly days—"Prepared" is your middle name.

c. Your headphones—you'll jam out on the bus ride home.

3. Your mom asks you to help her cheer up your Aunt Rose. You offer to . . .

a. give Aunt Rose a call and chat about her week.

b. spend the day organizing Aunt Rose's home office.

c. write a short story about your favorite family camping trip with Aunt Rose.

4. Your birthday party is next month. You . . .

a. don't know what you're going to do, but you've already invited your friends!

b. have the whole thing planned: theme, food, fun—you're ready.

c. created unique, hand-made invitations.

5. Your school planner is . . .

a. sprinkled with notes from friends.

b. neat, easy to read, and color-coded.

c. covered in sketches and doodles.

6. You find out you're going to have a new baby brother! You . . .

a. immediately call your best friends—they're going to freak out.

b. offer ideas about where to put the crib and rocking chair in the nursery.

c. start knitting a soft blanket for him—it's going to be adorable.

7. To prepare for a stressful day at school, you like to . . .

a. walk to class with your best friend—she's a really good listener.

b. make a to-do list so you feel like you can tackle anything.

c. dance out the nerves in your bedroom before leaving. Music always helps!

Answers

Super Social: If you picked **mostly a's,** you're a social butterfly. When you speak to a crowd or even just a few classmates, people listen. You get your point across in a way that's easy to understand and do a great job of getting others excited when you talk about something important to you. Raising awareness about an issue comes naturally to you because you're such a great communicator. You might excel at hosting a party that benefits an important issue, spreading the word about your favorite causes, and speaking at fund-raisers.

Down to Business: If you picked **mostly b's,** you're an organizer. You're not afraid to make a plan, roll up your sleeves, and take action. When you're tackling an issue, you like to be prepared and efficient. Sometimes that means making a list of everything you need to do before the end of the week, and other times that means meeting with your school principal to get all the facts before creating a game plan. You might thrive while starting a new club at school that focuses on an important cause, setting up a craft sale or event, or putting your planning skills to use in other exciting ways like collecting blankets for an animal shelter.

All About Art: If you picked **mostly c's,** you lean toward creativity when you're problem-solving. Big ideas come to you when you're doodling, making pottery, or listening to music in your bedroom. Creativity helps you connect with people, and you love using your artistic skills to tackle important issues or bring happiness to others. You'd shine while creating fun pins or signs for a march, playing music at a nursing home, or starting a blog or video series (with a parent's permission).

So, were you **Super Social**, **Down to Business**, or **All About Art**? Or do you see yourself in all three? Some changemakers are really great at one helping style, and some are comfortable with two or even three. We're all unique—activism can look a little different for everyone.

game-changing girls

Here are real girls who are making the world a better place. Can you figure out if they are Super Social, Down to Business, or All About Art? Remember—they might be strong in two or even all three approaches!

Ruby C. used her voice to make a difference.

When Ruby was eight years old, she started helping out at nursing homes in Arkansas where her mom works. Ruby volunteered and created art with the residents at the nursing homes. "I made hearts with their fingerprints on a canvas," explains Ruby.

When Ruby turned twelve, she watched a resident at a nursing home lose her dog because she could no longer afford to keep it. This made Ruby feel really sad. "I felt like I had to do something to change it." Ruby asked the residents, "If I could bring you any three things in the world, what would they be?" Ruby and her mom bought all the items they could with their own money. Then they turned to social media for some extra help.

"People really wanted to help the residents," Ruby explains. Ruby and her mom also posted about the project on a fund-raiser website. She wasn't sure what to expect. She thought, "Would I fail? Would anyone care? I'm glad I went for it." Ruby has raised more than $250,000 and continues to raise money for her cause. "Don't be afraid to use your voice," she says. "Don't forget the people right in front of you."

Gitanjali R. saw a problem and built something to help fix it.

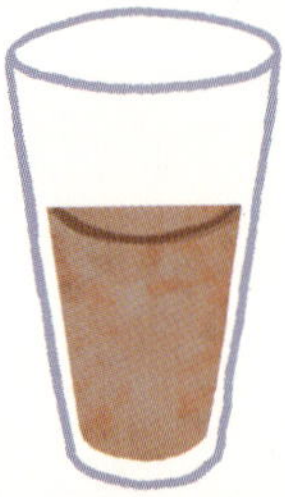

When eleven-year-old Gitanjali found out that thousands of people in Flint, Michigan, were drinking water contaminated with lead, even though city officials had told them it was safe, she was determined to help.

"Water is a valuable resource," she says. "It was shocking to see how many people, including kids my age, were affected by this huge, huge problem." She researched the topic. Then she came up with an idea to create an inexpensive and easy-to-use water testing device.

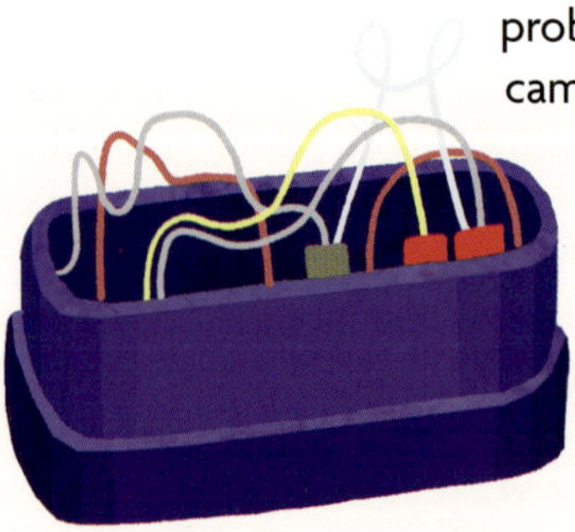

She brainstormed designs, drawing her device on paper. Then she built a model with cardboard. She worked in a room at her house that is devoted to homework and science projects.

Gitanjali entered her idea in a contest for young scientists. As one of ten finalists, she worked with a mentor to transform her idea into a working device, which won the contest.

Eleven-year-old Bria loves to paint and draw. She also loves wild animals. When she was eight, she painted a picture of a lion and won an art contest sponsored by a wildlife conservation group that protects animals and their habitats.

The experience inspired Bria to use her passion for painting to help wild animals. So far, she has sold more than 100 pieces of art. She's painted wolves, whales, tigers, cheetahs, and manatees. She donates the money she earns to organizations that help endangered species. "They need our help," she says. Many species might face extinction and disappear forever.

Before launching an art project, Bria studies at the library to learn about the animal she wants to paint. When she finishes a painting, she writes a description of the animal and takes a photograph of her painting. Then, with help from her mom, she posts her artwork for sale online. She's raised and donated almost $36,000 since she started. "We can all do little things to make our planet a better place for people and animals," says Bria.

empathy, always

When things start to feel too big or too frustrating (and that can happen when you're an activist), take a deep breath and remember how important empathy is.

Having empathy means trying to understand someone else's feelings and having compassion for them. It's the ability to put yourself in someone else's shoes to understand their point of view and what they might be going through. Empathy is what connects us to one another and our world, and it's what inspires us to take action to try to ensure that everything and everyone is happy, healthy, and safe.

This big, beautiful world we live in is made up of an endless variety of people, creatures, environments, and habitats. We look different, act different, practice different religions, speak different languages, come from different cultures and countries, and have different perspectives. But empathy reminds us that we're all living on the same planet. And our differences make us unique and beautiful.

When you practice empathy and compassion for others, you are changing the world. You're more likely to be kind, patient, and loving with your words and actions if you truly value the planet and everything and everyone on it. By opening your heart and mind to diverse perspectives and experiences, you are sharpening your empathy skills and being the best activist you can be.

CARING FOR A CAUSE

OUR Earth Matters
We all should CARE
#Cure CANCER
SERVICE DOG

what's important to you?

Is there an issue burning in your belly? Does it make you want to do something?

Maybe you love spending sunny Saturdays at a river near your home but have recently noticed trash everywhere.

Or someone you love has an illness and you want to raise lots of money to benefit research to help find a cure.

Maybe you saw a news story, and it really struck a chord with you.

Or you learned that many girls around the world don't get to go to school, and that's all you could think about for the rest of the day.

Maybe you got the reading list for the school year and you noticed the characters in the books all look the same, which might make some of your class-mates feel left out.

Maybe a family friend is going through a tough time and you really want to find a way to brighten their day.

Maybe you've noticed people being bullied because of their race, religion, gender, or something else and you want to educate your classmates about how to make everyone feel welcome at school.

It could be you're not sure why you want to help, but you do. That's OK too! Turn the page, and we'll figure it out together.

Complete these sentences and see if they spark an idea.

I'm very good at

____

____

____

____

It makes me really sad to see

____

____

____

____

If I received $1,000 to donate to a cause, I'd give it to

I get angry and frustrated when I think about

____

____

____

____

I'm passionate about

I feel warm and happy when I think about

____

____

____

Seeing

makes me want to do something.

I feel strong when I

____

____

It makes me happy to help

When I speak about

I feel really proud of myself.

beyond the bubble

We often surround ourselves with friends who are a lot like us because it's more comfortable. But we grow so much when we have new experiences, explore other perspectives, and ask questions. It can be fun discovering more about people we don't know.

Take some time to explore and think. Look around your home, venture into your community, and learn more about the world. You might find a volunteer opportunity you never knew existed right down the street!

discover more

Here are some ideas to expand your outlook:

Speak with classmates and friends who come from different backgrounds than you. There's so much to learn about the world from other people!

Read books, articles, or magazines about topics you know nothing about.

Watch a documentary or show about an unfamiliar country.

Listen to podcasts that discuss something new or different.

Ask a parent if you can research topics online.

Sometimes it feels as if the way we've always done something is the "right" way because that's all we know. But there are so many ways to experience the world. We're all unique, and that's what makes this big planet—and all its people—so beautiful!

what are you passionate about?

We all have different interests, passions, hopes, and dreams. Take a look at the list below and put a check next to anything that you're passionate about helping or impacting.

At home and school

- ☐ Stopping bullying
- ☐ Recycling
- ☐ Fighting racism or sexism in the classroom or on the playground
- ☐ Tutoring classmates
- ☐ Feeling safe in the classroom
- ☐ Making sure everyone feels free to be themselves

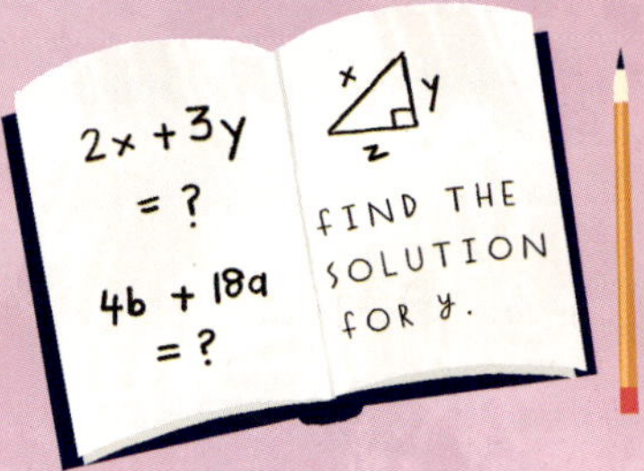

In the community

- ☐ Homelessness
- ☐ Rescued dogs or cats
- ☐ Helping elderly people
- ☐ Clean water for everyone to drink
- ☐ Making sure public spaces are accessible to everyone
- ☐ Helping kids who don't have enough to eat

In the world

- [ ] Climate change
- [ ] Helping after natural disasters like hurricanes, tornados, earthquakes, and wildfires
- [ ] Certain diseases or disorders
- [ ] Protecting the oceans
- [ ] Endangered species
- [ ] Education for all kids

More ideas:

Write down more ideas that come to mind in your Changemaker's Notebook. Remember the **How to Help?** quiz on page 18? See if you can pair your passions with your answers from the quiz.

Here are some examples:

You're passionate about making sure people in wheel-chairs can have fun at the city park.

+

All About Art

=

Design posters that let people know which areas of the park need to be more accessible for people in wheelchairs.

You're passionate about stopping bullying.

+

Down to Business

=

Set up a lunch meeting or club at school to show support for kids who have been bullied.

You want to help after a natural disaster like a wildfire.

+

Super Social

=

Ask your principal if you can speak at a school pep rally about organizations helping those in need after a wildfire.

Your classmate was diagnosed with cancer and you want to show support for her.

All About Art

Set up a time for kids in your school to get together and make cards for her.

You want to support your local food pantry.

Down to Business

Organize a day when someone who works at the pantry comes to your school to speak and explain which items are especially needed during the holidays. Then help collect those items.

There are so many causes to consider. What issue are you going to focus your attention on? After you choose, there's a lot to discover.

study up!

It's important to research the issue you want to focus on. Find out as much you can about the cause. Document what you discover in your Changemaker's Notebook!

Let's say you're really passionate about helping animals. When you begin your research, jot down all the ways animals need help.

Big Ideas

- Lots of dogs and cats need homes.
- Many endangered animals are on the verge of extinction (disappearing forever).

WHITE RHIN

- Climate change is affecting the habitats of many creatures.
- Elephants are killed for their ivory tusks.

- Poaching (illegally hunting wild animals) is a big problem in many countries.
- Some companies test products on animals.
- Pollution is affecting bodies of water, and this hurts dolphins, orcas, and other sea creatures.

Narrow It Down

Did one topic stand out? Narrow down your passion even further so you know where to start your research—you can always go back to the broader topic later.

Let's say you're really passionate about helping endangered animals, but orangutans hold a special place in your heart.

Dig Deeper

Use the skills you learned from **Discover More** on page 35.

- Read books, articles, or news stories about orangutans.
- Watch documentaries that feature orangutans and their habitats.
- Listen to an activist standing up for this issue. Who is shining light on orangutans?

"The future of the planet and humanity is in our hands."
–Dr. Jane Goodall

- Listen to podcasts about orangutans.
- Read about orangutans on a wildlife conservation site.
- Find others who share your interest in orangutans or other endangered species.

According to the World Wildlife Fund, orangutans are critically endangered.

- Talk to someone involved with the cause. Maybe there's an orangutan expert at a nearby zoo or wildlife organization you can reach out to.
- Chat with friends or teachers at school about orangutans. Your science teacher might have more information.

Researching the issue you're passionate about can lead you to amazing discoveries. Maybe you'll stumble on an organization dedicated to orangutans. Maybe you'll connect with a local leader hosting a fund-raiser in your city for orangutan habitats. There's so much to uncover!

GETTING STARTED

Equality
RUN FOR RESEARCH
MARATHON
MARATHON
OOD BANK

one action at a time

Maybe you're thinking, *Whoa, there's so much to tackle—I'll never be able to do all the things I want to!* That's OK—remember the pebble from the beginning of this book? Small actions can make a world of difference. Even sitting with someone who's alone at lunch or truly listening to a friend when they share something important with you can create ripples bigger than you ever imagined. Taking action at home or at school can change the world!

Look back at the research you did on the topic you care about. What are some small actions you can take every day to help make an impact?

Let's again say you're determined to help save endangered orangutans. Here are some ideas to make a difference at home or school, in your community, or on a global scale. You can apply these ideas to the cause you care about.

At Home and at School

Share an article about orangutan conservation with your family, friends, and classmates. Raising awareness is a great first step.

In the Community

Whip up a batch of homemade lip balm with coconut oil instead of palm oil. (The palm oil industry causes deforestation, which hurts orangutans!) With permission, sell the lip balms in your community, such as outside a store or at a craft bazaar. Give each customer a pamphlet about how to avoid palm oil in everyday products.

On a Global Scale

Write a letter to a company that disappointed you by destroying orangutan habitats. Explain why you will not buy its products and what you'd like the company to change.

Keep brainstorming! And remember, sometimes a small action turns into something bigger than you ever thought possible.

small actions, BIG changes

Global, community, and daily issues can all impact one another. Want to see how they're all connected?

Landfills in the United States are overflowing with clothing. What's an easy way you can help prevent this problem?

Daily action: Instead of buying lots of new clothes, buy items secondhand and pass down used clothes to younger family members or neighbors.

Community action: Organize clothing swaps to encourage people to share items they no longer need.

Global change: Throwing away fewer clothes prevents landfills from growing.

Fighting for equality for girls and women seems like a humongous, impossible issue. How can you get started?

Daily action: Use uplifting language when you talk to other girls. Compliment a classmate on how smart, confident, or creative she is.

Community action: Find other kids (and adults, too!) who care about empowering women. Form a group to talk about the issues facing your community.

Global change: With your group, organize a fund-raiser that supports a worldwide women's organization you love.

School can feel scary when you face bullies and lockdown drills. How can you help make schools feel safer?

Daily action: When you notice someone insulting a classmate or threatening violence, tell her or him it's not cool. If the bully doesn't stop, or if you feel unsafe, tell your teacher, school counselor, or principal.

Community action: Write a letter to local officials about how students feel at your school and what laws you'd like them to change. With a parent's permission, you might even attend a march or walkout that brings media attention to your issue.

Global change: Eventually, elected officials won't be able to ignore you and other kids fighting for what you believe in. Hopefully, the laws will change for the better, even if the change feels slow.

Small, daily actions can make a world of difference.

Quiz

where in the world?

Will you lend a helping hand at home, in your community, or globally?

1. You just listened to an incredible podcast about your hero and can't wait for others to hear it. What do you do first?

a. Run to your sister's room and hand over your headphones—she's going to love it, too.

b. Ask your teacher if you can tell your class about the podcast—some of it relates to your art history unit.

c. Share a link to the podcast in your digital school newsletter—you can reach tons of people that way.

2. For a school project, your teacher wants you to interview someone about her dreams. Who do you reach out to?

a. Your mom—she just opened a bakery and has lots of awesome ideas.

b. The mayor of your town—you'd love to learn more about what her dreams and goals are for your hometown.

c. Your pen pal in Spain—you've mostly written about school classes and your favorite color. What are her wishes and dreams?

3. It's your best friend's birthday next week, and you want to craft her something special. You . . .

a. make a pretty box for her favorite trinkets with supplies you find in your kitchen cupboard.

b. sign up for a local pottery class and make her a speckled ceramic mug.

c. watch step-by-step videos that show you how to sew a design she'll love in an embroidery hoop.

4. An article you read explains that many kids your age can't afford to play sports because equipment, tournaments, and fees are so expensive. What do you do?

a. Look around your home for gently used tennis rackets, soccer cleats, and basketballs to donate.

b. Sell wrapping paper or treats to raise money for your school's sports programs.

c. Host a sports-themed dance and ask everyone who attends to make a donation. Donate the proceeds to a sports scholarship organization.

5. The student council is organizing a walkout at school next week to show support for a cause you care about. How do you participate?

a. Spread out all your art supplies on the kitchen table to make posters and buttons—these will help your classmates get their message across.

b. Come up with five quick facts about the cause and share them with classmates. They'll be more likely to join the walkout when they know more about the issue.

c. Reach out to a local news station so it can send a reporter and camera crew. You can make a bigger impact if you can get the word out!

Answers

Mostly a's: Home is where your heart is. You're always ready to help your parents, siblings, and pets. There are lots of ways to make a difference starting right in your own house. The changes you make in your home and lifestyle can turn into ideas that grow and grow into something much bigger.

Sarah Q. **is changing the world right from her home.**

Sarah and her little brother, Liam, love animals. "That's why we're so close," she says. Together, they play with their dog, Cooper. Liam also likes to help squirt Sarah's horse, Monkey, with a hose.

"He laughs a lot when the animals are around," Sarah says. Recently, the thirteen-year-old worked at a summer camp that pairs therapy animals and kids who have disabilities, like Liam, who has Down syndrome. Therapy animals often provide comfort to kids with disabilities. "Petting, brushing, and leading an animal around makes Liam feel good," she says.

Sarah loved the camp so much that she started researching therapy animals so she could train her own. She saved more than $1,000 by babysitting and working at the camp. Then she convinced her parents to let her bring home a special miniature donkey.

"As soon as I saw Jupiter, I knew he was the one," she recalls. "He was so cute and gentle." Now Sarah is training Jupiter to do tasks he'll need to perform as a therapy animal, like wearing a halter, standing quietly for brushing, and ignoring noise.

"Sometimes he's stubborn—he is a donkey, after all. But he's so sweet and gentle," Sarah says. "He loves it when the kids rub his ears."

Mostly b's: You're connected to your community. You like to keep tabs on what's happening locally—at the park down the street, at the animal shelter, and at school.

Skylar T. is an activist who cares a lot about her community.

Skylar loves stuffed animals. "They are always there to comfort you," she says. When she found stuffed animals in a pile of things that her mom wanted to clear out of the basement, the twelve-year-old decided to find the animals a good home. She discovered a local organization that gives stuffed animals to cheer up kids in emergency situations.

Around the same time, Skylar's school asked students to do community service projects. Skylar wondered if other kids had gently used stuffed animals to donate, too. She talked to her teachers, made fliers, and set up a collection box at school. Skylar collected more than 300 stuffed animals, including a lot of bears, dogs, and pandas and a few frogs and boa constrictors.

Making the donation felt great, she says. The hardest part was deciding what to donate from her own collection of stuffed animals. She kept a few favorites but donated a pink pig. "He was a very special animal," Skylar says, "but I thought another kid might need him more than me."

Mostly c's: Going global is at the top of your mind! You think big and want to help people all over the world. Sometimes the world can feel huge and unreachable, but the internet makes it easier than ever to learn, connect, and spread the word about important causes.

Naja and Suri S. **were dedicated to going global.**

After ten-year-old Naja and her eight-year-old sister Suri heard about the destruction in the Bahamas after a hurricane, they wanted to help, especially because their great-grandma lives there. The violent storm had ripped homes apart, including blowing the roof off their great-grandmother's house. "I felt scared because we didn't know if Grammy was OK," Naja says. Their great-grandma was OK, but the girls wanted to help others who weren't.

The two sisters got busy helping long-distance. They emptied their piggy banks to help buy bottled water and tarps. After the supplies were delivered to the island, the girls continued to help.

Naja raised money to buy blankets. Suri held a toy drive at school. Their older brother collected clothes. Over the holidays, their family drove to Florida and then took a boat to the island. They delivered six crates of toys, 100 blankets, and 60 boxes of clothes and other supplies. Naja enjoyed handing out the donated items to island residents. "It was nice to see them smile," she says.

Suri says she loved helping with her family. "All the kids' toys were destroyed, and Christmas was coming," she says. "I'm only eight years old, and I felt like I made a big difference."

A HELPING HAND

There are countless ways to put your passions into action!

volunteering

Use your skills, talents, and time to give back.

Share your musical talents at a nursing home.

Train a service dog.

Sort cans at a food pantry.

Clean up walking trails at a park.

Rake leaves for an elderly neighbor.

Here's an example of an incredible girl volunteering:

Thirteen-year-old Shayla Y. began volunteering at a veterans retirement home when she was six. While volunteering, she noticed how hard it was for some of the veterans to use technology. She really wanted to help, so she volunteered to lead a workshop where she taught the veterans how to better use their cell phones.

Want to volunteer but aren't sure where to start?

With a parent's permission search for local organizations that match your interests.

Look for an e-mail, phone number, or volunteer form on the website, and ask some questions.

Ask about specific volunteer positions at the organization, and choose one that you think you'd be able to help with.

Learn to Read
Concord NH

To our readers,
Here is a list of volunteer opportunities at our organization. We need your help to:

- ☐ Collect books for a classroom
- ☐ Work at an after-school reading program
- ☐ Listen to younger students read
- ☐ Read your favorite book to kids during kindergarten story time
- ☐ Help out with a library program
- ☐ Make cool reading pins to hand out at an event.

Please mark how you can help, and return this form to the address above with your contact info.

raising awareness

Make your voice heard and spread the word.

Join or start a club at school to discuss important issues.

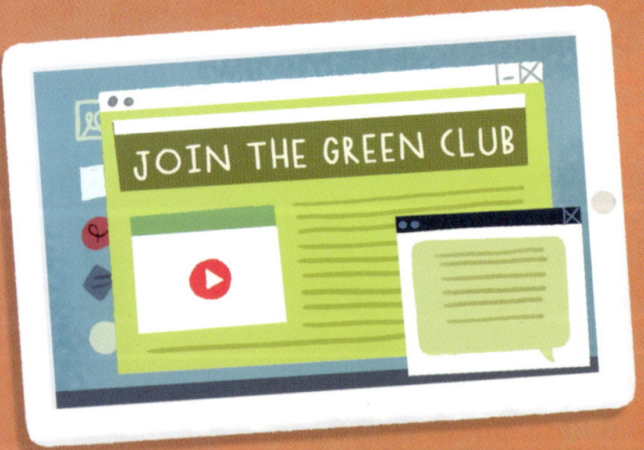

With a parent's help, write a blog or create a newsletter to spread the news.

Share your passions with friends and family.

Write a letter to the editor of the local newspaper about an issue in your community.

Attend a city council meeting about a problem that matters to you, and share your concerns.

Read about this activist who's speaking out:

When nine-year-old Riley M. tried to buy a pair of basketball shoes from one of her favorite athlete's shoe lines, she noticed that they were offered as a product only for boys. "I was disappointed and felt like it was unfair," says Riley. "I was upset because girls should have the same options as the boys." So Riley took action by writing a letter to the famous athlete explaining how she felt. He responded publicly and promised to make the change. He also asked Riley to help him design the sock liner for a shoe that was released on International Women's Day 2019. "By simply using your voice, you can make a change. You never know what could happen!" says Riley.

Have you ever thought about sending a letter to the government or to a business about something that's concerning you?

Here's how you might write a letter to a company about an important issue:

Address the person you're writing to.

State how you discovered the problem and start with a compliment—this helps make the reader more willing to listen to your suggestion!

Dear Mr. Smith,

I love the clothes you sell at your store—they're so soft and cozy. My brother and I have been shopping there since we were really young.

The last time we were in one of your stores, I noticed that the clothes in the girls' section were only pink and purple. I really like pink and purple, but I also like spaceships and dinosaurs like the ones on the shirts in the boys' section. Plus, my brother would love a pink shirt with a unicorn on it, but he couldn't find anything like that on his side of the store. It would be great if the kids' clothes weren't in separate areas for girls and boys. Then it would be easier for us to find what we like best.

Thank you for your consideration. I really appreciate it.

Best,

Serena Blake, age 10

Explain what you'd like to change.

Thank the person for taking the time to read your letter.

donating

Donate your own things and collect items to donate.

Gather needed items for a food drive or for a food pantry.

Collect clothing and donate it to a resale store whose profits benefit a charitable organization.

Donate gently used toys to a kids' organization.

Gather blankets or towels for a humane society.

Collect socks for a shelter for people experiencing homelessness.

Meet a girl who started a collection for a cause she believes in:

Bethany C. discovered that kids in a school in Alabama didn't have crayons in their classroom. She talked to her teacher and launched a plan to collect art supplies. Bethany spread the word at school to her classmates and teachers, and soon people started dropping off crayons in her classroom. She has collected and donated coloring books and more than 100,000 crayons to kids in need all over the world.

how to start a collection

Follow these steps for a successful collection drive:

1. What are you going to collect? Has a local organization put a call out for specific items? If not, reach out to local charities or organizations to see what items they need. This is an important step so you're not collecting something they don't need or cannot accept.

2. Spread the word! Tell friends and family members you're collecting items. Make fliers or posters, share a blurb on your school website, and ask your principal if you can make an announcement at school.

Tip: Some restaurants and companies will help if you ask! They might provide a discount to shoppers who donate needed items to your collection, or they might put out a collection box.

3. Be clear about where you'd like items dropped off and when. Will your teacher allow you to keep the items in your classroom? Is there a space at home where you can store them, such as a basement?

4. Donate your items and thank everyone who helped. What will you collect next?

fund-raising

Here are some fun ways to raise money for your cause.

Sell food or crafts to help your cause.

Participate in a 5K run or walk and ask friends and family for pledges to raise money for a cause.

Organize a dance in your community and sell tickets to raise funds.

Ask guests to make a donation to your favorite cause instead of bringing you a birthday gift.

Ask local businesses, artists, and makers to donate goods. Then host a silent auction and donate the proceeds to a cause.

Here's how one girl is raising money for an important cause:

Amiah V. learned that some families at her school couldn't afford to pay their cafeteria lunch bills, and that made her really sad. The six-year-old and her little sister wanted to help, so they sold lemonade and raised the money to pay the bills. But she wasn't finished—she and her parents kept fund-raising online, and they sold more lemonade. After a few months, they raised $23,000 to pay school lunch debts throughout Amiah's school district.

raise money creatively

A sale is a great—and fun!—way to make money. These tips for holding a craft sale can be adapted to just about any type of sale, from cupcakes to plants to used books.

Decide what you're going to craft, and practice your skills. Consider asking a friend to join in!

Decide where to hold your sale. Here are some ideas:

- At a table you set up outside your home on a sidewalk
- At a local business or coffee shop (call to get permission first)
- At school
- At your place of worship
- At a local college

Price the items and include a note that all proceeds go to charity.

Spread the word about your beautiful craft. Send an e-mail to friends and relatives, contact your local newspaper, make posters, text a photo of your craft to friends and ask them to pass it along, or send postcards to local businesses. The sky is the limit!

The first day of your sale, make sure you have everything you need:

Donate the money to the cause you're supporting, and plan your next sale! How can you improve? What parts of your sale went smoothly? What might you do differently next time?

ready . . . action!

So, volunteering, raising awareness, starting a collection, or fund-raising? How will you take action?

1. Your friend is overwhelmed because she's moving to a new apartment next week and needs to pack her and her little sister's whole room. You . . .

a. offer to invite a few friends over to help, and thank them with a yummy treat!

b. help her put things into four piles: trash, recycle, keep, or donate. Lots of organizations need gently used items!

c. offer to stop by and roll up all her winter sweaters—you're really good at that.

d. send her a blog or video with packing tips—those always help you get started on a project.

2. You're so excited for this year's school play, *Leaders Throughout History*. To get involved, you . . .

a. ask to be the event coordinator. You want to help with everything from planning the night to handling the tickets.

b. gather costumes to borrow from your classmates—you're going to be the costume designer.

c. offer to help choose which leaders to showcase—you want to make sure lots of people from different cultures and backgrounds are represented.

d. ask to be in charge of advertising—you want to make fliers in English, Spanish, and Hmong so that everyone in your community knows about the event.

3. Your school basketball team is raising money so you can all travel to the state capital for a tournament. What will you do to help?

a. Sell candy and donate the earnings.

b. Collect donations after games.

c. Organize a basketball clinic for younger kids—the proceeds go toward the trip!

d. Submit an article to your city newspaper to spread the word.

4. Your little brother is saving up for a new book, and you really want to help. You . . .

a. help him bake cookies and sell them to your friends and family. He can use the earnings to buy the series!

b. lend him your favorite book to read while he saves up.

c. offer to help him with extra chores so he can earn a bigger allowance.

d. call a used book store and ask if it has any copies of the book.

5. Every summer you and your family attend the community art fair. This year the art fair is struggling with money and needs some help. What do you do?

a. Reach out to businesses and ask if they'd be willing to make a donation to the fair.

b. Print out and donate some of your photography—the fair can keep the proceeds!

c. Volunteer to work the help desk—you're good at answering questions.

d. E-mail a beautiful piece of artwork from last year's fair to your friends and family and explain that the fair needs some support (don't forget to give the artist credit!).

Answers

If you answered **mostly a's,** you're ready to raise some funds. Here are some ideas to get you started:

- Put on a play or variety show with your friends. Donate the money you make from selling tickets.
- Host a silent auction and donate the proceeds.
- Hold a bake sale and donate the money to a cause you believe in.
- Host a car wash with your friends or teammates and donate the money.

Return to page 70 for more ideas about how to fund-raise.

If you answered **mostly b's,** you're a committed collector. Try these tips:

- Collect handwritten cards from your friends and donate them to a nursing home or hospital.
- Collect eyeglasses and donate them to a local organization or mail them to a large one.
- Donate gently used books to your community center.
- Collect hats, mittens, coats, and other winter apparel to give to a shelter or local organization.

Head back to pages 66–69 for more ideas on how to start a collection or donate items.

If you answered **mostly c's,** you're very into volunteering. Here are some tips to jump in:

- Coach a little kids' sports team.
- Plant trees with an environmental organization.
- Clean cages at an animal shelter.
- Offer to run an event for kids at your local library.

Flip back to page 58 for other volunteering ideas.

If you answered **mostly d's,** spreading the word is your specialty. Here are some ways to begin:

- Make posters, pins, stickers, and T-shirts to get the word out.
- Give a presentation to your class about an important issue.
- Start a podcast with a friend and talk about the issue.
- Send creative e-mails to your friends and relatives about your cause.

Return to page 62 for more ideas about raising awareness.

EASING YOUR WORRIES

EDUCATION FOR EVERYONE
Women's Rights
Clean Water
WAR
POLLUTION
LGBTQ rights

where to start?

Once you start using your changemaker skills, you might become aware of more issues. Sometimes it can feel like there are problems everywhere you look.

Things are happening at school that don't seem right (maybe someone tugged at your head scarf or made a disrespectful comment about your hearing aids).

You overhear your parents talking about homelessness in your city.

You hear a leader or an activist taking a stand about an issue (like equal pay or women's rights) on the news.

You see commercials on TV about dogs and cats who have been abandoned.

You read an article about climate change.

A friend is being teased at school for how she looks or dresses.

Trash is filling our oceans and hurting sea creatures.

It's easy to get overwhelmed sometimes. When that happens, it's important to take a break and care for yourself.

take care of you, too

When you feel overwhelmed, here are some ways to take care of yourself:

Talk to a parent about how you're feeling.

Go for a walk.

Chat with a friend who is a good listener.

Do something that brings you joy. That might be listening to music, playing your favorite sport, doodling, or watching a favorite movie—whatever makes you happy!

Move your body—run, dance, do some cartwheels!

Cuddle with a pet.

Rest before jumping back in.

Sometimes you can't take a break from the issue you're fighting for, especially if it's affecting you personally. For example, it can be tough to step away from your efforts to stop bullying at your school if bullies are targeting you. It's really hard to think about making change when your own safety is in question.

In some cases, you'll need help, especially if you're in an unsafe situation. Reach out to an adult you can trust, such as a parent or school counselor. Making a difference often means asking for help! You deserve to feel safe and cared for, too, no matter what issue you're fighting for.

If you need help in the moment, deep breathing can be a great way to take a quick, refreshing break. Go to a private place, like a bathroom, close your eyes, and take deep breaths for five minutes. Imagine a place that makes you feel calm, or think of a happy memory.

Spread Too Thin

It's impossible to help with *every* issue.

It's great to care about many issues, but no one has the energy, time, and space to tackle them all. You can't save the world by yourself!

When you're overwhelmed, you might feel tension in your muscles, not sleep well at night, or have trouble concentrating in class. These are signs that you've gotten involved in too many projects. It's OK to put some things on hold and start back up when you feel ready. If you're volunteering with a group, explain to the group leaders why you need to take a break. You can always join again later.

To make the biggest impact you can, choose one or two issues that you're very passionate about. When you have time, you can help your friends with issues that mean a lot to them, too.

THE FUTURE IS YOURS

dream big

Close your eyes and think about incredible women making a difference in the world. Who comes to mind?

All of those leaders started where you are right now—wondering what they could do to make the world a better place.

Remember the pebble in the pond? All these great leaders started small, but their ripples spread positive change across the world.

Will you join them?

get started!

Where to begin? Here are some ideas!

Daily Difference

- Sit by someone who is alone at lunch.
- Share an article about an issue you care about with your family.
- Truly listen to a friend when she shares something important with you.
- Write a nice note to a parent.
- Bring a treat to a friend or classmate going through a difficult time.
- Pick up trash at your school playground.
- Offer to help a classmate with a subject he's struggling with.
- Help out around the house without being asked.
- Leave spaces nicer than you found them.
- Tell your school custodians how much you appreciate them keeping your school a happy and clean space for learning.

- Compliment someone's hard work.
- Carry a neighbor's groceries up to her apartment.
- Help your siblings with their homework.
- Shovel a neighbor's driveway or sidewalk.
- Leave a note with a kind message for someone to find on the bathroom mirror at school.

- Write thank-you cards to your teachers.
- Join your school student council or community service club.
- Make a snack or meal for your younger siblings.
- Draw a picture for or write a thank-you note to your mail carrier.
- Pet-sit for a friend or neighbor.
- Send a text to a friend or relative telling her how much she means to you.

- Don't jump to conclusions about people (you don't always know what they're going through).
- Ask someone what pronouns they use.
- Grow flowers in your backyard and bring a bouquet to a friend.
- Hold the door open for someone.
- Tidy up a common area in your home without being asked.

- Be open-minded to new experiences and ideas.
- Carry a water bottle instead of using plastic bottles.
- Rake leaves for an elderly or sick neighbor.

- Wear a shirt that shines light on an important issue.
- Give someone a second chance.
- Put yourself in someone else's shoes and really try to understand how she feels.
- Lend a friend your favorite book.
- Eat less meat, if you're able. (It takes 2,500 gallons of water to make a single pound of beef.)
- Give a school presentation about a cause you believe in.
- Wear used clothing instead of buying new.

- Bake cookies for a neighbor or friend—just to brighten their day!
- Stand up for classmates being bullied.
- Listen to someone when they need to work through a problem in their life.

- Smile and say hello to a student at school you don't know very well.
- Print as little as possible—save those trees!
- When you notice someone doing a great job or being a good friend, tell her!
- Use reusable bags at the grocery store.
- If you're able, bike instead of riding in a car!

Community Caring

- Attend a neighborhood meeting to talk about an issue that's important to you.
- Write a thank-you note to a community hero.
- Volunteer to collect needed items for a local women's organization.
- Drop off towels at an animal shelter.
- Write an article in your school newspaper about an issue that could be improved (such as more signs written in Spanish for students who don't speak English).
- Collect socks for a local shelter for people experiencing homelessness.
- Ask a parent if you can pick up litter on a nearby hiking trail.

- Plant a tree.
- Volunteer to tutor a younger student.
- Buy fruits and veggies at a farmers market.
- Donate canned goods to a food pantry.
- Sew or knit blankets for newborn babies.
- Make a meal for a family going through a difficult time.
- Pick up trash and recyclables at a state park.
- Hold a yard sale with friends and donate the proceeds to a charity.
- Donate board games or toys to a hospital.
- Read to little kids at your local library.
- Volunteer to plant flowers at a local park.
- Surprise firefighters or police officers with baked goods.
- Put on a performance or sing a song at a children's hospital or senior center.
- Support local business owners and artists by buying their products, food, and art.
- At your next birthday party, ask friends to bring donations for a favorite charity instead of gifts.
- Attend an event hosted by a charity you support.

- Write a letter to the city council about an issue in your community (such as needing more lights on a poorly lit sidewalk).
- Make birthday cards for senior citizens at a nursing home.
- Donate gently used books to a day care center or after-school club.
- Check for babysitter, first-aid, or CPR trainings in your area that allow kids to be certified.
- Collect books, sports equipment, clothing, toys, and board games for a group home for kids who are in foster care.
- Volunteer at an organization on a holiday that your family doesn't celebrate so that other volunteers can have the day off.
- Learn American Sign Language or another language to better communicate with friends who might not speak English as their first language.
- Raise money to purchase gifts for a family in need during the holidays.
- Grow out and donate your hair to an organization that makes wigs for kids who need them.

Go Global

- Make a poster for your cause and hang it up at school after checking with the principal.
- Buy goods or gifts made by women around the world.
- Tell your class about a global issue that matters to you.
- Write a letter to a company that disappointed you by treating its workers poorly. Explain why you're not going to buy or use the company's products and what you'd like it to change.
- Sell bracelets at school and donate your earnings to a worldwide organization you love.

- Write a letter to the president about an issue that worries you.
- With a parent's help, start a blog or video series about an issue you believe in.
- Attend a march dedicated to an issue that's important to you.

dive in

Are you ready to get started, changemaker?

Begin in a way that makes the most sense to you. Maybe that means dipping a toe in the water by listening to a podcast about an issue you don't know much about. Maybe it involves wading in and attending your first nature club meeting at school. Maybe you are ready to dive right in and run a fund-raiser in your community.

You have everything you need inside you, whether you start big or small. It's time to take the plunge!

Do you have an activist tale to tell?

Write to us!
Making a Difference Editor
American Girl
8400 Fairway Place
Middleton, WI 53562

Here are some other American Girl books you might like:

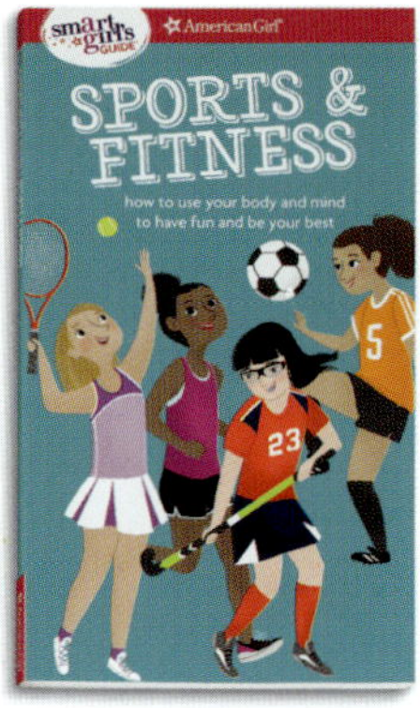

Each sold separately. Find more books online at americangirl.com.

Parents, request a FREE catalog at **americangirl.com/catalog**.
Sign up at **americangirl.com/email** to receive the latest news and exclusive offers.

play@ American Girl™

Discover online games, quizzes, activities, and more at **americangirl.com/play**